AF824152

RETIRE IN PEACE

RETIRE IN PEACE

how to achieve the retirement you deserve

M Andrew Riddle

ISBN-13: 9780692782828
ISBN-10: 0692782826

Table of Contents

Preface

Too often, the only way to learn is through experience, and since you only live once, those lessons learned cannot always be applied "next time." You only get one shot at things like raising your children or planning your retirement, and there is simply no way to know everything you'll eventually wish you knew. This reality, however, is often a good thing because it leads you to the one and only course of action: moving enthusiastically and optimistically forward.

Fortunately, diving into something yourself does not mean you must do it alone. While we may personally lack experience in a certain subject, there are others out there with valuable experience we can draw from to make the going easier on our own journey. I'm in my early 40s. I have a wife, two kids, two dogs, and by way of full disclosure, I've never retired. That said, I have more experience with retirement than any individual retiree possibly could.

You only get to retire once, and your experience will be limited to your own retirement and perhaps that of your close friends. My firm, on the other hand, has helped many people retire. We've taken that journey with all sorts of different people from varying backgrounds and diverse walks of life. We've seen what works and what doesn't. We've seen which conventional wisdoms are conventional for a reason, and which conventional wisdoms routinely fail. We've seen the markets through many and various upheavals and political leadership changes, and we've seen what they can do to a retirement nest egg—both good and bad.

We've seen people at the beginning of their retirement when they are playing golf, traveling, meeting grandchildren who are just being born, and having a grand time. We've seen them in the middle of retirement when golf and travel get harder and those grandchildren don't come by quite as often. And we've seen them toward the end, when life seems to revolve around doctors and ever-changing living arrangements. The hurdles faced in each phase of retirement are different. The mental, emotional, and financial support needed will change too.

This short book hardly has all the answers, but it has a few points of guidance I hope you'll take to heart. They represent the journey of many retirees, and there will be similarities in their journeys and your own. The words in this book are mine, as I had the privilege of writing them, but the lessons to be shared are most certainly "ours" and for that reason this book is written in the third-person. My friend and business partner, Justin Streeter, and I have learned a lot about retirement in our many years of helping others retire. It is my sincere hope that our experience will help you retire in peace.

Introduction

The word "retirement" is overused, and often misused, in our modern lexicon. Tennis players "retire" from matches if they become injured. Racing drivers "'retire" from the race when their engines break. And people "retire" from jobs with great frequency. None of these things are what we typically mean when we use the word "retirement," and are certainly not what we mean when we use the word in this book. These events are more aptly described as resignations—quitting something because you're unable, or unwilling, to go on.

The retirement we talk about in this book is not an event, but rather a stage of life in which earning a living ceases to be a primary motivation for your daily activities. The beginning of retirement is marked for many people by resigning from a job, but that action is largely symbolic. For many, the shift in mindset into retirement occurs before they actually resign their last job. What is critical about the shift into retirement for your finances is that you no longer intend to pay your expenses from monies earned by your daily work. Instead, you intend to rely on your fixed income and savings to finance your life.

The word retirement often conjures notions of people sitting on their front porch, sipping coffee, and watching the world go by. In truth, retirement has nothing to do with your level of activity. In fact, we find that many of our clients are busier in retirement than when they were working. One of our clients left his corporate job to start a new company with his son and take a teaching post in a local executive MBA program. In terms of his financial planning and investment planning, we consider him retired because he is no longer trying to earn a living from his daily efforts. Yet, he is busier now than he ever was before.

Another of our clients had a highly successful consulting practice. In fact, he came to be in such high demand that he made a fabulous living taking just two to three consulting jobs per year. Typically, he and his wife spent six months of the year traveling recreationally. He decided to retire and not take any more consulting jobs. Instead, he followed his passion to a local nonprofit where he works 30 hours per week as the Director of Public Relations. He will be the first to tell you he is working more hours in "retirement" than he did before he retired, but the point of his work has changed. He makes very little money in his current role and donates back most of what he does make. He is working quite a bit, but he isn't working to make a living. So, for planning purposes, he is retired.

Retirement also bears no relationship to your age. It's certainly true that many people enter the retirement stage of their lives in their 60s, but that's more a function of how long you need to work to get your kids out of the house and prepare for retirement than anything else. We have clients who achieved wealth early in life and fully retire in their 40s. They are quite active, of course, and some of them work hard at various endeavors, but the motivation for working isn't to make a living.

Retirement is a stage of life, and thanks to modern medicine, it is a stage of life most people enter into while relatively healthy and vigorous. In our experience, the majority of retirees aren't ready to just sit in a rocking chair and watch the world go by. They are interested in continuing to live life and have fun. They view retirement as an opportunity to live their lives more fully than ever before. Many of our clients work at jobs they love (rather than the ones they had to have to pay the bills): they play golf, volunteer in the community, travel the world, and do many other things they didn't have time for when they were working.

This book discusses having a successful retirement. It's about making that last quarter of your life as purposeful and fulfilling as possible by removing one of the major roadblocks to a successful retirement: finances. If you have saved enough for retirement, the advice in this book will certainly be easier to implement. We believe that ANYONE, no matter how poor a job they did as savers in their working life, can have a successful retirement. Obviously, the less you saved, the more sacrifices you may have to make to find success, but with some good directions, you can get there from wherever you are today.

1

The Concept of Retirement is Born

Retirement, if you think about it, is sort of an odd concept. At a time in our lives when we are typically healthy, our kids are out of the house, we have more knowledge in our jobs than anyone around us, and we are less inclined to climb tall mountains or sail the high seas than we might have been before, we resign from our job. We call it quits. When we probably have more to offer our employers in terms of time and experience than we've ever had before, we walk away.

Not only do we walk away, but society expects us to. There seems to be a general belief that senior citizens should stop working, so younger people can gain employment and middle-aged people can assume leadership. Think of it as the life cycle of the American workforce. Where did this modern notion of retirement come from?

The concept of retirement finds roots in the Social Security Act of 1935, which is either the greatest piece of social policy developed by any nation or the worst government handout idea ever conceived, depending on which news channel you prefer. What is interesting, though, isn't really whether Social Security was a good idea or a bad idea, but how profoundly it has impacted our modern view of work. Everyone today, no matter their view on Social Security or their political leanings, expects to retire in comfort. There may be disagreement on how retirement should be funded, but there is almost universal agreement that everyone ought to retire. That universal agreement would actually come as a great surprise to our ancestors and to the proponents of the Social Security Act of 1935.

Retirement, as it were, didn't particularly exist prior to 1935. In fact, earlier definitions of the word suggest it meant "to move to a quiet place for meditation and worship." It had nothing to do with winding down one's working life. With no public benefits system, with very few people eligible for pensions, and with many people still self-employed across various industries including agriculture, most Americans simply worked until they could work no longer, relying on family for support in their final years.

The Social Security Act gave birth to the idea that people should end their working lives and maintain a minimal standard of living. Retirement in 1935 was no picnic. The average life expectancy in 1935 was only 61.7 years, and the average retiree spent less than 10 years in retirement. Even with Social Security benefits, most Americans continued to live their final years in relative poverty.

In 1935, a form of retirement was certainly born, but it was hardly the modern notion of retirement that we hold dear today. Retirement in 1935 was designed to be a safety net for the elderly and nothing more.

2

The Evolution of Retirement

The complexion of retirement began to change in the 1940s when General Motors installed one of the first modern pension plans. As other companies followed suit and increasing numbers of Americans moved out of self-employed agriculture jobs to work in the factories of new mega-corporations, retirement became something to look forward to for employees. Rather than continuing in laborious factory jobs into old age, workers could retire with a pension supplemented by Social Security and maintain a standard of living very similar to the one they had while working.

The Employee Retirement Income Security Act of 1974 did much to secure pensions for employees. With growing comfort in their retirement income and an evolving notion that retirement was a time workers had earned and should enjoy, the average retirement age in the United States declined steadily from the 1950s, when it was approximately 67 years of age, through the middle 1990s, when it dropped as low as 62.

While the average retirement age continued to fall through the middle to late 20th century, the average life expectancy of the American worker rose, thanks primarily to advancements in modern medicine. People were living longer in retirement than ever before, but with their retirement income guaranteed by their former employer and the United States government, workers were unconcerned with how to replace their paychecks in retirement.

It was in this era that our modern notion of retirement really began to take shape. In the 1930s, Social Security provided a safety net that made retirement possible; pensions from the 1940s through the early 1980s made retirement desirable. Companies used the pension plan as an employee-retention tool. In exchange for an adult life of service, the company would provide a satisfying retirement income for the employee. Retirement became a time of life to look to with anticipation and became a "right" of the American worker: something earned through years of loyal service.

This "right" mentality toward retirement was very different than what was contemplated by proponents of the Social Security Act in 1935. At that time, some 30 million senior citizens in the United States lived in poverty. Social Security was designed to ensure that those people had food and a place to live. It certainly was not designed to be a reward for a lifetime of hard work. Social Security did generate the seed that grew into our modern notion of retirement. The company pensions of the 1940s through the early 1980s drove our modern ideal of retirement: workers deserve to retire from work at some point prior to their being unable to work any longer and maintain a standard of living similar to the one they had while working.

3

Retirement Today

In the mid-1980s, pensions began to give way to savings plans like 401(k)s, moving the burden of saving for retirement away from the employer and placing it squarely on the employee. The 1990s brought the earliest retirees who were at least partly funding their own retirement through their 401(k) savings. Of course, in the 1990s, the stock market was racing upward and people were very optimistic about the economy and their retirement. A Gallup Poll in 1995 revealed that the average American expected to retire at age 60 and that 50 percent of American workers planned to retire by age 65.

Unfortunately, the optimism of the 1990s gave way to a harsher reality. The first wave of workers to have 401(k)s or similar self-funded plans as their primary retirement vehicle are now retiring, and it appears most of them have not saved enough. According to a study commissioned by *The Wall Street Journal*, conducted by the Center for Retirement Research at Boston College, and published in 2011, "the median household headed by a person aged 60 to 62 with a 401(k) account has less than one-quarter of what is needed in that account to maintain its standard of living in retirement."[1]

Gallup polling suggests that this fact is not lost on American workers. In 1995, American workers expected to retire at age 60. In 2016, American workers do not expect to retire until age 66.[2] In 2014 Gallup polling, more than half

---

1 http://www.wsj.com/articles/SB10001424052748703959604576152792748707356

2 http://www.gallup.com/poll/191477/three-workers-foresee-working-past-retirement-age.aspx

of American workers feared outliving their retirement savings, making it the top economic concern among American.[3]

Statistics suggest that the fear of outliving retirement savings is quite real. More than 60 percent of retirees in 2011 retired without a pension, relying mostly on their 401(k) savings and Social Security. According to the 2007 *Period Life Table* published by the Social Security Administration, a person who retires at age 65 can expect to live, on average, 20 more years. To put that in perspective, the average American worker who retires at age 65 will spend nearly a quarter of their entire life in retirement. No wonder 2014 polling tells us retirement is America's top financial concern.

3 http://www.gallup.com/poll/168626/retirement-remains-americans-top-financial-worry.aspx

4

So Now What?

It's true that many Americans today are employed in office jobs rather than the typical physical labor jobs of the 1930s and 40s. And it's true that, because of that, people probably can work longer now than they could then. It's also true that federal law has reacted to much of the age-based downsizing of the 1980s and 1990s, making it illegal to fire someone simply because they are over a certain age, giving seniors a chance to stay employed longer.

Even with these changes, working forever is not much of a plan. Modern medicine has done wonders to extend life, but it is not necessarily equipped to preserve a standard of life and keep us healthy enough to work forever. And whether any of us want to admit it, as we age, technology and ways of doing business eventually begin to pass us by. For almost all of us, retirement is inevitable, and living a relatively long life in retirement is equally inevitable.

This inevitability is one our ancestors would have cherished. We find ourselves in an odd place in the early 21st century, where many approach retirement with as much dread as anticipation. The good news is you can have the retirement you deserve. All it requires is a little effort, a moderate amount of discipline, and a lot of planning.

At our firm, we have helped many people retire and learned a lot about it along the way. The goal of this book is give you some insight into the life-altering event that is retirement and share some thoughts on what will make you successful.

5

Defining Success

Every journey must begin with an end in mind. To paraphrase the Cheshire Cat of literary fame, if you don't know where you are going, then any road will do! So, when we say you can be "successful" in retirement, what do we mean?

Let's first start with what we don't mean. Success in retirement has nothing to do with your current standard of living. One of the core values of our firm is that we take our clients as we find them, and we don't judge their past financial decisions. If you are retiring, your savings are what they are, and you either saved enough to maintain your standard of living or you didn't. We have a lot of great planning and investment tools at our disposal, but a time machine isn't one of them, so there is no point in looking backwards and wishing you had done things differently. A retirement plan can only look in one direction: enthusiastically and optimistically forward.

Success, then, is a prospective proposition. Based on where you stand today and the means available to you, there is a retirement that will meet some or all of your retirement goals and is ambitious enough to be satisfying, yet realistic enough to be attainable. For many people, that means mapping out all your retirement goals and then assigning them some priority.

One of our clients was tragically widowed in her early 50s. She had a good job at a major Atlanta-based corporation and retired at age 62 with a modest pension and some 401(k) savings. Her two children had grown up and moved out of the house, and she came to us for help planning her retirement. We started by asking her to list all of her retirement goals. The ones that bubbled to the top included seeing the world (she had never really travelled), doing mission work with her church, spending time with her children, and keeping the family home.

We took those goals, started putting costs to them, and it quickly became apparent that meeting all of those goals on her income and savings was going to be a challenge. So, we asked her to prioritize and began looking for ways to meet the most important goals. Through the planning, it became obvious that keeping the family house was going to require sacrificing the other goals. It was very large and expensive to maintain, was in a country club community that required significant monthly dues, and still had a fairly substantial monthly mortgage obligation attached to it. Moreover, the unpredictable expenses of homeownership did not fit into the way she wanted to manage her financial life in retirement.

So she sold the family home and rented a very cool condo near the top of a tall building in a trendy part of Atlanta at half the cost of the old mortgage. Between reducing her monthly living expenses and boosting her savings with the equity from the sale of her home, traveling the world recreationally and meaningfully contributing to her church mission trips became a reality. When the real estate market crashed in 2008, we negotiated a decrease in her condo rent, and she was able to rent a second condo in Charlotte, North Carolina, just minutes away from her daughter and newborn granddaughter.

In giving up her country club home, many would say she reduced her standard of living in retirement. In fact, many of her former neighbors expressed sympathy at her "giving up" the country club lifestyle. But the truth is that she is enjoying exactly the retirement she wanted. She has explored the far corners of the world, made great new friends, learned bits and pieces of many languages, spent time in other cultures, and even recently launched her own travel blog. She's one of the happiest people we know and will tell anyone who cares to listen that retirement is a wonderful stage of life. Anyone that meets her can feel her enthusiasm for life. Is her retirement "successful?" Absolutely.

Did she have to prioritize and sacrifice some goals to achieve others? Of course she did, but that is what planning is all about.

Success is fundamentally about being happy in retirement, but that's too esoteric a definition for most people—and, really, it's too esoteric to be useful in the planning process. So rather than define "success" as happiness, let's call happiness the purpose of the retirement plan. Success is balancing your goals and aspirations against what can be done realistically based on your income and savings, and then living that plan to the fullest. Failure is living too far above or too far below your means in retirement. You don't want to go broke; you also don't want to leave more of your aspirations unfulfilled than you have to.

Successful retirees find that balance, create an ambitious yet realistic plan, and then get on with the serious business of enjoying the life their plan offers them. Successful retirees don't worry about outliving their money because they have a plan to guard against that outcome. Retirement plans look only in one direction: forward to a bright future. Success in retirement is realizing the bright future that you map out today; it has nothing to do with how you used to live.

And the best news of all? Anyone can be successful in retirement, no matter how much or how little they saved while they were working. So keep this definition of "success" in mind as you read this book. This isn't a contest to see who can have the most toys between you and your neighbors or who can take the most lavish trips. It's about finding the balance between your goals and your means that gives you a peaceful, stress-free, yet exciting and purposeful retirement.

6

The 10 Tips

TIP #1: RETIRE *TO* SOMETHING, NOT *FROM* SOMETHING

So this isn't exactly a financial tip (we promise the next 9 tips are), but we've witnessed this up close too many times to not make it the first tip of the book.

We work with a lot of retirees and feel compelled to report that not all of them are happy. That may not surprise you, but it might surprise you to learn that it has nothing to do with money. We have clients with very high net worth who are completely set for retirement and are miserable. We have clients on a very tight budget, taking more investment risk than they would like in order to try and stretch to the goal, who are loving life and having fun.

The difference between them? Some of them retired *from* something, others retired *to* something. One of our clients was a high-level executive at a Fortune 50 company. He was a man of great importance. He had a staff of people who worked only for him. He had an office on a very high floor of a very grand building in downtown Atlanta. When he needed to travel for business, which was often, his assistant arranged for the company limousine to take him to the company plane so the company pilot could fly him wherever he needed to go.

One day, he was "that" guy. The next day, he was the subject of a lavish party and much adoration. The day after that, he was retired. A new person had taken his place, and the company didn't need him anymore. For the first couple of years of his retirement, he traveled the world with his wife, caught up with his kids and grandkids, and generally had the retired life television commercials have convinced us is nirvana. But once the newness wore off, he was bored. There weren't any more meetings to go to. There weren't anymore big decisions to make. There weren't many people asking for his advice or seeking his leadership. It suddenly dawned on him that he had truly retired from something he really liked—his job—to nothing at all. Free time is great when you're busy. When all of your time is free, it loses its value. You need something to do that really engages you, that makes getting out of bed in the morning worthwhile, and that gives a purpose to your life. Many people find it after they retire as our client ultimately did (he's now the Chief Operating Officer of a local nonprofit), but the transition will go much better if you can identify it before you retire.

Another of our clients was in human resources for a large company. She retired at the age of 68 and held on that long because she was very worried she hadn't saved enough to retire. But she had known for years what she wanted to do. There is a local nonprofit in her city that serves the working poor, providing them clothes, food, and financial assistance. Most of the client-facing work is done by volunteers, but to effectively volunteer, you have to be available during the day and you have to commit the time to learning the job. She had served on their board, but never in the facility.

The day she retired, she walked out of her office and straight to the nonprofit. She signed up and is now working there 20 hours per week. She doesn't get paid a dime, but she trains other volunteers, she's a valued resource for the paid staff, and she's touching the lives of countless people. She also plays Bunco, plays with her grandkids, never misses a performance in her local theater, and even swings by the office to visit us from time to time (though we usually have to beg). She's very happy and has been since the day she retired. Why? She didn't just retire *from* something, she retired *to* something that is important to her, that gives her purpose, and that keeps her engaged with the community. And yes, with a solid plan in place and a very reasonable level of investment risk, she had enough money to retire.

Retirees used to live to age 67. Now, if you are at retirement age, your life expectancy will take you into your 80s! This is a great opportunity to see the places you've never seen, make a difference in your community, perfect your golf game, learn to cook, or restore a car. Go enjoy retirement! But make sure you are retiring *to* something. You still need a purpose, a reason to get up every day.

TIP #2: HAVE A PLAN

You've probably already gathered that this is our top financial tip, but we cannot stress it enough. **You cannot be successful in retirement without a plan!** Your bills don't disappear just because you retired. Your car won't suddenly run forever just because you no longer have a paycheck. Your hot water heater will still break, the kids and grandkids will still want birthday presents, and the IRS will still expect your regular and significant contributions.

So how do you replace your paycheck? What rate of return do your investments need to earn over time so you can outpace inflation and maintain your budget? Is that rate of return realistic and, if so, what investments will get you there? If you need extra money for a cruise or a household emergency, is there a tax-free place to get it?

There are more items in the planning process than the space in this book will allow, but at a high level, you have to know your budget, you have to know how much income you need from your investments, and you have to know how often you need to receive that income. Then you need a plan for how your investments will produce that income, and you need to know how long your money will last based on those assumptions and some realistic assumptions about inflation.

Planning must drive all of your financial decisions in retirement. A solid plan should drive your investment decisions, budget, insurance needs, and estate planning. Planning also has to remain evergreen. Your plan needs to be reviewed at least annually and certainly upon the occurrence of any major events. For our clients, we review their plans annually and actually redo the entire plan every two to three years to be sure we are still on course. Don't let anyone offer you investment advice (or any other sort of commission-generating advice) without first giving you a comprehensive plan that shows how their advice is going to help you achieve your goals.

We'd like to think it goes without saying, but in our experience it does need to be said, and sometimes often: stick with the plan. If you want to veer off course, then redo the plan to account for whatever it is you want to do and see if it makes sense. We run all of our plans to age 100. If our clients can't reach age 100 on paper, then we are concerned. If their money will get them to age 100, then we view them as being in the retirement safety zone. One of our clients, against our advice, took an early retirement in his late 50s. Our plan at the time he retired showed him running out of money at age 87. To try and improve the situation, we worked with him to develop a budget and a reasonable investment plan to give him some chance of lasting longer. In his early 60s, he decided he needed a boat. We revised the plan to account for that expenditure and to raise the budget to account for the expenses associated with the boat, and now he runs out of money in his very early 80s.

This client is always very complimentary and appreciative of our work. He refers his friends to us for advice and never finds fault with our analysis. He just doesn't like it, so he's hoping it will all just somehow work out. Maybe it will. Maybe the 1990s will return and he'll ride a huge market run-up into the retirement safety zone. Maybe he'll win the lottery or get a huge inheritance from a long-lost relative. Or maybe he'll run out of money in his early 80s. Hoping for the best is not a reasonable strategy. Have a plan and stick to it.

TIP #3: KNOW YOUR INVESTMENT RISK TOLERANCE

That brilliant financial plan you've crafted now has to be implemented. A major step in doing that is developing an investment plan that will provide the rate of return required in your plan, combined with a level of risk that is not only reasonable for someone in your particular situation, but is also a level of risk that you can live with. It all sounds easy enough, but there are some realities you have to know.

Risk and return are related, and at the end of the day, if you want more return, you have to take more risk. That means you have to be willing to stomach your portfolio value going up and down. Understanding why your portfolio is designed a certain way and understanding the fundamentals behind the investment decisions will help a lot, but there is a certain amount of gumption required on your part, particularly if your portfolio needs to stretch a little to accomplish your goals.

You aren't 45 anymore. Many new clients come in and tell us that they didn't panic when the recession of 2001 hit, and they didn't panic when the crash of 2008 happened, so they have a relatively high tolerance for risk. The truth is they probably did have a high tolerance for risk, but watching your 401(k) go up and down while you are still getting a paycheck every two weeks and retirement seems like something way off in the future is one thing. Watching your nest egg drop precipitously when it is all you have to live on is another matter entirely. Most people's appetite for investment risk goes down in retirement. Unfortunately, it sometimes takes a market correction for them to realize it, and then it's a little late.

Spend time with your advisor figuring out your true tolerance for risk. Yes, you need to hit some rate of return number in the plan, but you have to live through this plan too. It's a lot easier to start less risky and turn up the heat as you go than it is to start too hot and try to turn it down after your portfolio has lost a lot of value. Our advice is take your risk rating (we use a scale of one to five), and then go back at least a half position in your initial investment plan, just to be sure.

One other thing: if your advisor hands you a two-page worksheet produced by an annuity or mutual fund company with some questions that produce a nice and tidy risk tolerance score that just happens to align you with a particular investment, run for the door! Evaluating a client's risk tolerance is one of the hardest things we do. We spend a lot of time in meetings searching for that answer. We thoroughly review their past investments looking for clues, and even then, it's not until we've installed their first investment plan and lived with it for a while before we know for sure we have it right.

Start retirement with a less risky portfolio than you think you want, as it is much easier to add risk to a portfolio than it is to take it away. And keep in mind you'll likely be retired for 20 years or more. You don't have to get all of the investment return you'll ever need in year one.

TIP #4: MANAGE INFORMATION

Some of you have always been interested in the world financial markets and the technical parts of investing. Some of you have been hobbyists or do-it-yourselfers for most of your investing life. If that's you, then you have probably already learned to manage the never-ending stream of hysterical financial information pumped at you by media outlets who need you to keep watching and keep reading so they can sell advertising. But this isn't most of you.

In our experience, most people take an acute interest in investing for the first time at retirement. Better late than never, we say, but be mindful of the amount of information available and its sources, so you can judge its usefulness to your financial education.

Television is probably the worst place to get financial information. Guys banging on fake buttons and shouting about stocks you should buy is entertainment only. Television "journalists" are often worse. Fox News, CNN, MSNBC, they all know who is watching their programming during the day: You! That's right—retirees. And all of it is designed to hold your attention. They know retirees are highly interested in the world economy and world financial markets, and they know if they scare you enough, you'll keep watching. Television is not the place to find in-depth, objective analysis. It's the place to find sound bites and over-the-top opinions designed to create emotional responses and keep you tuned in.

If you really want or need up-to-the-minute information about how the markets are performing today and announcements from companies, television can be helpful. But if you seek thoughtful analysis, look elsewhere.

The print media is a lot better. Why? Because it's a lot harder to digest. You actually have to read and comprehend the writer's point. There aren't running tickers and headlines to distract you from what is being said. There is no breaking news to distract you from how completely asinine the last commentator's point may have been.

Sure, print media suffers from some of the same weaknesses as television in that print media does need you to read their product so they can sell advertising, but written publications tend to get an audience by being credible over a long period of time. Plus, the medium itself, writing, forces the writer to be more thoughtful, do research, and not just talk out of turn.

Nonetheless, even in the print media, you need to know who is doing the writing. Most major print publications covering the world of finance have a few established columnists that are "commentators." Typically, they are former journalists. While many of them are very good, keep in mind that they are getting paid to have an opinion. So, while they may provide some analysis and support for their position, like lawyers, they are paid to have a position. One of our clients, a talk radio personality, has explained it like this:

> As a commentator, you are almost never criticized by management or your audience for being wrong. You are also rarely credited with being right. What matters is that you have an opinion that is loud enough and strong enough that people will either completely agree or completely disagree with you because either way, they are engaged, which means they will keep listening and the advertisers will keep paying.

Many print publications will also publish the written work of academics, either regularly or occasionally. Academics perform the same role in finance as they do in other disciplines: they analyze data from a very sterile point of view and with no interest in the outcome of their research. They are scientists who seek to explain what they see going on around them. They are amazingly able to bicker with each other, write long dissertations about why others of them are wrong, and generally carry on as only academics can. Their work can be very thought-provoking and will typically be the most in-depth and thorough of all.

We follow several leading academics in the research we do at our firm, but there is one fundamental truth about academics you must keep in mind: they don't ever have to answer to a client or anyone else for being wrong. If they are completely wrong, the worst thing that will happen is they will be rebuked by another academic. So, while they typically do a lot of research and present cogent positions, they have no need to be conservative, or even practical, in their opinions.

Finally, many print publications feature articles or columns written by professional investment advisors. The publications and professionals have an obvious agenda of having readers hire them, but in many ways that forces them to be rational. Their clients will read what they write, so it better be consistent with how they work with clients and it has to make sense. They are also forced to be conservative because the repercussions to them for being wrong can be enormous. Thoughtful, independent advisors can be good sources of information and analysis, just don't confuse them with these guys.

Anyone can write on the internet and most of them do. The internet is filled with articles about why annuities are completely evil (written by fee-only planners), why annuities are the greatest investment vehicles ever conceived (written by annuity salespeople), why variable life insurance is a rip-off (written by life insurance agents who aren't allowed to sell it because they don't have a securities license), why variable life insurance is the single most important purchase you'll ever make (written by life insurance salespeople who happen to have securities licenses), and on it goes. If you look hard enough, you can find an internet article to support any position on any topic you can think of, and almost all of them are written by people with a vested interest in you agreeing with them.

Google is, in many ways, both the best and worst creation of the information age. The best part is you can gain access to answers to almost any question you can think of. The worst part is that filtering the information is completely on you. *The Wall Street Journal* won't publish just anyone; WordPress will. Know your sources.

Read a blend of commentators, academics, and professional money managers to get different perspectives. We always advise our clients to pick a couple of sources they trust and stick with them. As you read multiple pieces over time from the same set of writers, you'll begin to get a feel for writers whose thoughts and opinions seem logical and who view the world of finance through a lens similar to yours. One can seldom go wrong with *The Wall Street Journal* and *Barron's*, but there are also other good sources out there that are a little less technical and easier to digest.

How to judge other sources of information? There are some obvious things like looking at the qualifications of the writers and what their financial interests are in having you read their work. To us there is a more fundamental filter. Any writer or speaker who proclaims to know what you should do with your money, despite the fact that they have never met you, should be avoided.

TIP #5: CASH IS KING

This might strike you as the most obvious tip in the book, but we find surprising resistance to it from our clients. When we present a portfolio design to a client, one of the asset classes is always cash. The amount of cash always comes right out of the comprehensive financial plan we did before we began the portfolio design. By the time we actually install the investments, our clients have seen our recommended cash allocation at least twice and agreed to it at least twice. Invariably after the investments are in place they ask, "Don't we have too much cash?"

The truth is there is only one type of wealth that can actually be spent—and that is cash. Your cable provider won't take a share of a mutual fund in payment of its monthly bill. Toll roads don't take bond coupons. Whether it's exciting or not, you will need cash to pay your bills and live in retirement. Replacing your former paycheck can only be done with cash, and the best way to be sure you have cash when you need it is to always have cash on hand.

So the answer is no, we don't have too much cash in the plan. Cash prevents us from selling out of investment positions every time you want to go on vacation. Cash allows us to have buy and hold strategies in the investment portfolio. Cash allows you to sleep at night knowing we have a certain amount of time "sitting in the bank." And cash allows us to invest in assets beyond just stocks and bonds such as real estate, oil and gas programs, and business development debt that can be lucrative, but not always liquid.

Cash isn't just for emergencies or expenses either. Cash is critical for opportunities. What if you bump into that 1958 Jaguar you've always wanted? What if your daughter launches a great new business and you'd like to invest? What if you have an opportunity to make a major difference in your community? You'll need cash for this, and while cash can always be raised by raiding the investment account, that shouldn't be part of the plan. Having enough cash on hand to keep the investments intact for their allocated time horizons should be the plan.

So, how much cash? That depends on how much you can afford, but we like to see one year of living expenses in cold, hard cash and another two years in cash reserve type investments. Then every year, as you spend through the cold, hard cash, we move a year of cash from the short-term cash reserves and replenish them from maturing investments.

Trust us, cash is king. But you'll have to be strong on this. Your know-it-all friends and in-laws will mock you for having so much cash in your portfolio. Other advisors will tell you all of your money should be working at all times (because that is how they get paid). But you can just smile and nod, knowing that if 2008 happens again, you'll have cash to ride out the storm and allow your investments to return in value while your know-it-all friends are selling at the bottom to pay their bills. Cash isn't exciting, but it is definitely king.

TIP #6: EXPENSES DON'T GO DOWN IN RETIREMENT

Maybe this is less of a tip and more along the lines of debunking a really common myth, but it's a reality you have to deal with. Expenses very rarely go down in retirement. We have helped a lot of people retire and can tell you that only in very rare cases do people's expenses go down in retirement. And when they do, it's because those people very intentionally force them to. Most of the time, expenses in retirement actually go up.

Think of it like this. When you were working (or now if you are still working), did you spend more money on the weekends or during the week? The weekends, right? You went out to eat, you played golf, you went shopping, you went to the movies, and all of the other things you found entertaining or distracting. Monday through Friday, you went to work. Other than buying lunch, there isn't much opportunity to spend money on a workday. In retirement, you have seven-day weekends, which means more time to do what you enjoy, more time to travel, and more time to spend money. At least in the early years of your retirement, the recreation part of your budget will go up.

The rest of your budget will stay basically the same. The cable company doesn't give you a discount for being retired. Neither does your auto insurer, your electric company, or your mortgage holder. Your basic costs of living in retirement do not go down unless you intentionally downsize your life. It is true that retirement is more of a continuum than an event, and your spending habits will change. At age 65, you are likely to take a trip to Alaska. At age 85, you are more likely to read a book about Alaska, but you will also likely have increased medical and living expenses. For most of our clients, it's not a dollar for dollar trade. So, expenses do tend to go down over the course of retirement, but not precipitously and usually not at the beginning. So, plan accordingly.

TIP #7: BUY A BIG TV

You worked hard for a long time and retirement is a reward. You need to enjoy it. Your retirement resources are likely not endless, but their bounty is very much in how you view them. You need to view them as abundant, not scarce. We occasionally see clients who want to sell everything, live in a tent, and eat ramen noodles. Armed with a good plan, you know where you are, where you are going, and how you will get there. So live a little. If you want a big TV, go buy one.

TIP #7A: BUT NOT TOO BIG A TV

Your retirement savings will afford you a certain lifestyle, and hopefully it is one you are comfortable with. But very rarely will your retirement savings afford you a grander lifestyle than the one you had while you were working. If you couldn't afford a Ferrari while working, you probably can't afford one now. So go buy a big TV, but don't go crazy. That million dollars needs to last awhile!

TIP #8: DON'T FORGET ABOUT THE REST OF THEM

It's always interesting to bring up the topic of children with our new retiree clients and watch as their eyes either light up with pride at their children's accomplishments or immediately roll because their 28-year-old is still living in their basement. The good news about your children is that, as you approach retirement age, you likely know them pretty well and you know whether they are going to continue needing your financial support. If so, you need to make sure you are accounting for those expenses in your comprehensive financial and retirement plan. You will also want to make sure you've really thought it through in your estate planning. If your child is incapable of managing his or her own affairs, is dropping your six-figure nest egg in their lap going to be a good idea? And, by the same token, if your children are very responsible, successful adults, shouldn't you get rid of that trust you put in your will when they were in elementary school?

Make sure your planning matches the needs of your children and your desires for their future. We find that most of our clients are very resistant to including their children in any of their planning, even when their children fit the very responsible, successful, middle-aged adult profile. We don't push that issue, of course, as it's a very personal decision, but it can cause problems. Ironically, many of our clients who refuse to let their children know "any of their business" are the same people who suffered tremendously from a lack of information from their own parents.

Consider this reality: approximately 30 percent of parents receive some sort of financial support from their children. Think about that for a second: that is 30 percent of all parents in the United States. We know many adults today are underemployed or not employed at all. We know they have no savings, and we know they aren't planning for their own futures. Do you think the percentage of parents relying on their children for financial support is going up or down in the coming generations? Up, of course. And to get through that successfully, the generations of the family are going to have to start working together a bit more.

One of our clients is a very successful Generation X business owner. His parents, like many from their generation, were getting by on social security and a very small pension. His father was 67 and his mother was 61 at the time of his father's retirement. Like many parents, his parents refused to share any details of their financial life with him, so he could only assume all was well.

What he didn't know was that his parents couldn't afford health insurance for his mother who, at age 61, was not yet eligible for Medicare. And since they didn't tell him, he had no idea his mother was uninsured. Our client would have been happy to pay for a catastrophic risk-type health insurance policy for his mother. It would only have cost him a few hundred dollars per month, and he could easily have afforded it. But, his parents didn't give him that opportunity.

As you have probably guessed by now, his mother experienced some very significant medical problems that resulted in hospital stays and surgeries. With no insurance and no way to pay for the care she needed, our client had to step up. Because his parents insisted on keeping their financial life secret, our client wound up spending tens of thousands of dollars on his mother's care with no opportunity to plan for that expense and no insurance to help offset it.

This tip really should raise two questions in your mind. One is whether you need to share anything with your children. The other is what have your parents not shared with you? We all know how hard it is to get our parents to talk about their finances, but if your parents are living on a fixed income and have relatively little personal savings, they owe it to you to tell you how fragile they really are. Nothing throws financial plans off like the unexpected.

Our experience tells us that a large percentage of our retiree clients will encounter expenses related to their children and/or their parents' care, but we have no way of predicting which clients will be affected. As you begin mapping out your retirement plan, take a look at the people around you and see what is going to be required of you. Then figure out, realistically, what you are going to be willing to do. We hear a lot of tough talk about how parents aren't giving their 28-year-old a penny if he loses his job again. And then he loses his job again and our clients support him. Be realistic. If you know in your heart of hearts you will support your son and you know he's probably going to need it, then plan for it.

Most of us have loved ones, and we hope they will be there for us just as we hope we'll be there for them. But some of our loved ones are more dependent than others, and if you have some of those, then you need to be sure they are accommodated in your plan. Don't hope they won't cost you money in retirement. Go ahead and plan for those expenses. It will help ease the financial sting when they do need help, and it will give you some parameters about how much help you are willing to give. And if your parents are the great unknown, and for many of us they are, do what you can to learn more about their situation.

TIP #9: MAKE A NEW PLAN IN YEAR TWO

It takes 12 months before our clients know what it's like to be retired. It takes 12 months for them to know what their expenses really are, what income they really need, and where exactly it needs to come from. Since our plan is built around data gathered from them, until they really know, we can't really know. In year one we guess; in year two, we plan. So, no matter how careful you were in your initial plan (and the more careful you were, the better), you need to make a new plan in year two. And it will actually be your first plan.

TIP #10: PICK THE RIGHT TEAM

Actually, let's start with the more fundamental question: do you need a team? The answer is that it depends. If your retirement is built entirely around fixed income (social security and a pension), then you may not need much help, as your financial life isn't really going to change in retirement. You were used to getting a paycheck every two weeks; now you'll get one per month. If you were a responsible household budgeter before, then you can handle it now. Live within the means of your new paycheck, keep some savings for emergencies, and you should be in good stead. Taxes can become a bit more complicated in retirement, particularly if you do anything to earn extra income, so you might want to put a CPA on your team to help with your tax returns, but otherwise, you may not need much.

However, if part of your retirement income is going to come from your savings, typically a 401(k) or IRA, then your odds of achieving the retirement you deserve are greatly enhanced by having the right team of professionals around you. But who is out there and what should they be doing? Our goal here is to help clear up some roles, so you can be sure the bench is properly filled.

What you need is what is becoming more commonly known in the industry as "wealth management." Wealth management comprises at least the following disciplines:

- **Financial Planning.** This is the professional who will build the financial plan from the ground up and answer the big questions: How much money do you need per month/year to live in retirement? What rate of return do your investments have to achieve to satisfy your income needs? When do you need to be "paid" from your portfolio (monthly, quarterly, annually) and in what amount? How long will your savings last?

The Financial Planner is also the person who will be called on again and again to review course corrections. If you buy that boat, what does that do to the plan? Can you purchase a beach house or are you better off renting? If you decide to start paying your grandson's tuition, what does that do the plan?

- **Tax Advice.** Unless you were a business owner in your working life, you probably didn't have to pay quarterly tax estimates and really plan your taxes. As a retiree, you will, and tax planning will be critical. Tax return preparation is pretty easy to find, but what you really need is a CPA that will do tax planning. Being told in April what you owe is one thing. Being told in July what it looks like you'll owe next April is far more valuable and gives your Financial Planner a chance to plan for that expense.
- **Investment Advisor.** These professionals are incredibly easy to find, which is why finding good and honest ones is so difficult. But someone has to design and manage the portfolio, and unless you've done that professionally, this isn't something you want to leave to chance. A good investment advisor will assess your tolerance for risk, review the plan from the Financial Planner to understand the income and rate of return targets, and then design a portfolio around those goals.
- **Estate and Advanced Planning.** Everyone needs at least simple wills, powers of attorney, and healthcare directives. If you were fortunate enough to amass significant wealth during your working days, then you likely need advanced tax and estate planning. Advanced planning can help reduce your estate for tax purposes, protect assets, accomplish charitable goals, and provide for an orderly succession of your wealth.

There are different ways, of course, to go about building the team. The Bill Gateses of the world hire their team members directly and put them on staff, so they work for no one but them. It then becomes those people's full-time job to manage the wealth of their employer. Taking this as an ideal model, service providers began looking for ways to provide the same level of dedicated service to slightly less wealthy, but still very wealthy, clients, and the family office was born.

Family offices are often run by an attorney, though some are run by other types of professionals, and their primary function is to gather and keep data for you and to select and manage the members of your team. Good family offices limit the number of clients they will take (usually 10 to 20 clients maximum) and charge flat annual fees for their service. These fees can range from \$20,000 a year to more than \$100,000, depending on the level of service. These fees are above and beyond the fees charged by the team members (investment advisor, money manager, CPA, etc.). Family offices are a good solution for people who have enough wealth that they could hire their own staff, but not so much wealth that they absolutely have to. The family office lets them outsource that function so they don't have to manage it themselves, but still gives them a very high level of dedicated service.

For people who do not want the expense of the family office, the traditional solution is to pick each professional yourself. This allows you to have exactly who you want as each team member, but creates challenges for you as it puts you in charge of making sure each professional is in sync with all of the others. Did anyone ask the CPA before they sold those stocks and took the capital gain? Did anyone make sure the life insurance beneficiaries got changed after the lawyer implemented the trust? Did anyone ask the financial planner to calculate the required minimum distributions in the IRA before they took money from it? The difficulty for you isn't just making sure these people talk to each other, but knowing enough to be sure they are asking each other the right questions.

Ideally, you find someone who can quarterback the team for you. These days, most financial advisors hold themselves out as exactly that, and the better ones can certainly perform the role. Just be sure you know what you are paying for and how you are paying for it. A lot of financial planners actually outsource the investments. Some are more transparent about this than others, but you can easily end up paying anywhere from 2 to 5 percent per year in asset management fees and investment costs if you aren't careful. So, ask a lot of questions and be sure you understand the answers about how your money will be invested, who is really managing the money, and how much it all costs.

Also keep in mind that asset management fees and investment costs are sometimes two different things, particularly if an advisor is embarrassed about the total cost. If the advisor is going to put you in mutual funds, perhaps his fee is only 1 percent per year. But those funds often have another 2 percent (or more) of costs built into them. So you are really in for more like 3 percent. Ask enough questions to get a complete answer, so you can be comfortable and so you can compare the value proposition of different advisors.

However you choose to build your team, give it the time and consideration it deserves. Ask your friends and family for the names of professionals they use and, more importantly, ask what they like and don't like about the service they receive. Spend some time and effort choosing the right team, and you'll be rewarded with peace of mind. There is a lot to worry about in financial planning, investment management, and taxes. Spend your retirement doing the things that give you purpose and let your team do the fretting for you.

7

Planning for Retirement

You will be glad to hear there is more than one way to plan for retirement, particularly if you have ever made use of one of the internet's many retirement calculators. Most of those calculators attempt to determine exactly how much money you will need if your current expenses continue all the way through retirement and inflate over time. Not surprisingly, they typically calculate a depressingly large number. If you can hit that number or one like it, kudos to you! Your retirement should be very well funded, and you will likely leave a financial legacy to your kids or whomever else you choose. If you can't hit that number—no worries, as there is more than one way to plan a retirement.

Once you retire, your nest egg is what it is and your job becomes to manage that nest egg the best way possible. We say that to reiterate that we don't have a time machine you can borrow to go back and save more money. You and your nest egg will be moving optimistically and enthusiastically forward into retirement. No regrets and no looking back.

Managing your nest egg will typically fall into one of three strategies. If you have saved some but not enough to really impact your retirement, then your nest egg becomes a savings account. You will live off of your income (social security, pension, etc.) and use your savings to cover emergencies and opportunities that present themselves. If this is you, don't budget your way to spending 100 percent of your income. You need to save a few dollars every month, just in case, or that nest egg will run out before you are ready. This is how you lived while you were working, so you know you can do it.

If you have saved enough to meaningfully impact your retirement, and hopefully you have, then the question is how to manage the nest egg so that it provides you with regular income. If you are going to work with a professional, this is the point where you must make sure you understand the advice you're getting, because the answer to this question is a plan, not a product. To be perfectly clear, the answer to how you stretch your nest egg out over the rest of your life is not an annuity or some brilliant basket of mutual funds. The answer is a plan. How that plan is executed is something you will have to consider later, but not now. Right now, we need a plan.

There are two basic plan structures that will work. The ideal plan is what we like to call a "faucet." The less ideal, but equally workable plan, is one we like to call "buckets." Which one will work for you is a function of how much you've saved and how much you need to take regularly from the nest egg to maintain your chosen standard of living.

THE FAUCET

Imagine, if you will, a typical hot water faucet in your home. The more you turn it, the more water comes rushing out, but the faster you will drain the tank of hot water. The less you turn it, the less water comes rushing out, but the longer the tank will last. There is a "right" degree of open for the faucet that best balances your need for hot water with your desire to not run the tank dry too quickly. After all, no one likes a cold shower.

If you survived our tortured analogy, you have the gist of a faucet plan. In the ideal faucet plan, your retirement nest egg is large enough that the annual investment gains will offset what you are taking out as income, and the nest egg doesn't shrink. When you hear people talk about "living off their dividends," conceptually this is what they mean.

We say this is the ideal plan because running out of money shouldn't really be in play. If your withdrawals and your investment gains roughly even out, your nest egg should at least stay the same if not grow some during your retirement. This gives you the flexibility to spend more than you planned or to do some serious legacy planning for your children or the causes that interest you. A well-thought-out faucet plan gives you a lot of financial options going forward, and that is always a good thing.

So, how much can you take from your portfolio while executing a faucet plan? You will find great debate about this on the internet, but academia has long recognized a safe withdrawal rate as 4 percent. Of course, the less you withdraw, the safer the plan. But the nest egg doesn't do you much good if you don't use it, so 4 percent is the standard answer. To help with the math, if you have a $1,000,000 nest egg, you would expect to be able to take out $40,000 per year without drawing down the principal. Then, at the end of your life, you would expect the nest egg to be the inflation-adjusted equivalent of $1,000,000.

That last bit is critical, by the way. Inflation is the enemy of your faucet plan. If you need $40,000 per year from your nest egg today, you will likely need much more than that 15 years from now to maintain the same standard of living, due simply to inflation. The only way for your income to grow is for the nest egg to grow because we want to keep the withdrawal rate at 4 percent. To simplify, let's say inflation one year is 3 percent, and your nest egg grows by 7 percent. You withdrew 4 percent per the plan. So, at the end of the year, your nest egg is 3 percent bigger than it was at the beginning of the year. Have you gained anything? Not really, because you withdrew the investment return, but the nest egg has kept pace with inflation. Next year, you will be getting 4 percent of a slightly larger nest egg, which should help offset the rising prices of groceries, gas, and the other things you consume.

When this works over a long period of time, the actual amount of your nest egg will grow, but its buying power should stay basically the same, which is why you need to stay disciplined about your withdrawal rate as it grows. We know there is a temptation to increase the withdrawal rate when the market has a big year. Don't do it. Stick with your 4 percent. That 4 percent is going to give you a raise anytime the market pushes your nest egg up, but if you over-withdraw in good years, you will have to under-withdraw in bad years, and we don't want that.

The reason the 4 percent might feel low is because we want to use it to establish a floor for your income. If you started at $1,000,000 and you were taking $40,000 per year in income, you don't want to cut your income to something less than $40,000 per year. If you feel like you have to, then you likely fell victim to sequence risk, namely the risk of bad investment years happening at inopportune times.

Bad years will happen in the stock market, and it is very difficult to predict which years they will be. Unfortunately, it matters greatly to your faucet plan *when* the bad years show up. If they hit early in the plan, they can be very disruptive. If they hit in the middle, they are less of an issue. If they hit at the end, they don't usually matter much at all. It is important that you push the potential bad years out as far as possible, and you do that by starting your faucet plan with cash. Each $40,000 you can leave in cash is a year you don't have to withdraw from the investments, which means it's a year where things can go wrong without causing too much pain.

Just keep in mind the targeted withdrawal rate of 4 percent. When you finally turn the faucet on somewhere down the road, you don't want to be taking more than 4 percent, so you can't leave too much in cash or you won't have enough money working for you. But, you do want to leave enough in cash that you give your nest egg a buffer against a bad year in the markets hitting right as you are moving into retirement.

When you were saving, did you ever hear of "dollar cost averaging?" You likely did, but to remind you, dollar cost averaging is buying into the market regularly to take advantage of pricing differences. If we put $12,000 into the market one day, we will find we either bought at a good moment or a bad one. If we put $1000 per month into the market for 12 months, we will find we bought at all sorts of different prices and hopefully some of those prices were low to bring down the average cost of our investments.

We remind you of this because regular withdrawals from your nest egg are the other side of the dollar-cost-averaging coin. Whatever good dollar cost averaging does for you in market declines (you are paying less for stocks), regular withdrawals do damage in the opposite direction, as you are regularly withdrawing from a shrinking pot of money. You can adjust for this, of course, by withdrawing less, but your monthly expenses don't decline just because the market is going down, so that isn't a great answer.

The better answer is to maintain your minimum withdrawal, say $40,000 per year, no matter what the market does. To do this successfully, you need an answer for the sequence risk posed by a nasty turn in the market in your first couple of years. Once your nest egg gets some growth into it, the inevitable down year isn't as scary.

There are other risks in a faucet plan, just like any plan that includes investments. The two big ones to look out for on the front end are inflation and sequence risk. You must be sure your faucet plan accounts for inflation over the long haul and also accounts for market risk in the early years.

Please remember, this is planning; there is no product that does this. You need a plan that you're comfortable with and you understand before you consider any sort of investment vehicle. Once you have a faucet plan and have the kinks worked out, then there are a lot of different directions you can go with your investments. Some people like to build a portfolio around dividend-paying stocks and other income-generating investments and use the cash produced by the investments to fund the withdrawals. Others prefer to buy growth-oriented stocks and tactically sell each year to produce the cash to cover the income. Still others like to blend those strategies.

And then there are whole host of products on the market that claim to execute faucet plans for you. Annuities are the most common example, many of which promise you a particular income stream for the rest of your life no matter how the stock market performs. These products eliminate sequence risk, but sometimes exacerbate inflation risk. Used improperly, they also create liquidity risk, which is simply the risk that you need your money and you can't actually have it because it is tied up in the annuity.

We are purposefully not going to editorialize about annuities here. They are tools like anything else and can be used properly to people's advantage or abused for the broker's advantage. You'll have to decide for yourself whether you need the guarantees of the insurance company to sleep comfortably at night and not worry about your money. Our only two cents is that you should seek a second opinion if you meet with someone who suggests you put all of your money into an annuity or a series of different annuities.

THE BUCKET PLAN

The faucet plan is great if you can do it, but as you undoubtedly noticed, it takes a lot of money and a relatively small withdrawal rate to make it work. Remember though, its major upside is that running out of money is not part of the plan. If you start with $1,000,000, you should end with the inflation-adjusted equivalent of $1,000,000 or something close to it.

The bucket strategy, on the other hand, is a plan designed to stretch your nest egg to its limit. If you've heard someone glibly say, "I plan to spend my last dollar on my last day," they are (hopefully) executing a properly constructed bucket plan. The upside of the bucket plan is it will greatly stretch your retirement savings and give you more income than your savings would give you in a faucet plan. The downside, of course, is that running out of money is a risk of the plan. You should do all you can to guard against that, of course, but it is a "spend down" plan by its very nature, and if you are spending down the nest egg, there is always going to be some risk that you outlive your savings.

The major variable in a bucket plan is your life expectancy. A faucet plan doesn't care how long you live. In theory, you could live indefinitely and not run out of money in a faucet plan. A bucket plan is aiming for you to spend down your nest egg, so it matters greatly what age the plan uses as an end point. You can run your bucket plan out to age 110 just to be safe, but you may find that the income that gives you doesn't work for your life. If you can bucket plan to age 110, you can usually faucet plan with similar results.

For bucket planning to really work, you have to pick a more realistic ending age, and that invariably invites in the risk of outliving your money. As you go through the planning process, you'll see that even a one- or two-year change can make a big difference in the plan. Faucet planning is fun; bucket planning isn't because consideration of your mortality is inevitable. If you are 70, play golf every day, don't take any meds, and your parents lived into their 90s, you better pick 95 or so as your ending age for planning purposes. If you are 70, take heart medicine and are substantially overweight, using 95 as your ending age is likely to just reduce your standard of living unnecessarily.

A version of bucket planning, by the way, is how pensions manage their money. The advantage of the pension is they are dealing with large numbers of lives, and they can work on averages for life expectancy. You are dealing with two lives at most, you and your spouse, and that isn't enough to draw statistical conclusions. You will be forced to confront your own health and lifestyle and make a guess about how long you will live. You should add a few years to it, of course, but the ending age is the most critical variable in the bucket plan.

Once the ending age is established, the number of years you will live in retirement is then broken up into "buckets." For example, you retire at age 65 and you plan to age 95. This gives you 30 years in retirement that you might break into 3 buckets that each hold 10 years. Why buckets? Because we like analogies!

Consider the bucket as holding the amount of money you need for 10 years. To comfortably get through those 10 years, the bucket must be full. But, and here is the brilliance of bucket planning, it doesn't have to be full today. It has to be full when you need it. So, the bucket for the first 10 years will be filled with a lot of your retirement nest egg, as you will be spending from that bucket right away. The second bucket, however, you won't be touching for 10 years. That gives the money you put in the second bucket 10 years to grow through investments. So you don't need to fill that bucket up today at all. You just need to put enough in there today that it can grow to be full in the next 10 years. And if that sounds like a good deal, consider the third and final bucket that you won't be touching for 20 years! You will be putting even less money in that bucket today, as it will have 20 years to fill itself up through investment growth before you need it.

The other major advantage of bucket planning is that it allows you to take more investment risk as long as you keep that risk in the right bucket. You shouldn't take a lot of risk in the first 10-year bucket since that is the money you need now and in the near-term future. Can you take more risk with the money you don't need for 10 years? Absolutely. And can you take more risk still on the money that you won't be touching for 20 years? Of course you can. And the more risk you can take on those buckets that you won't be using anytime soon, the less money you have to seed them with today.

Bucket planning can work very well if you've selected an appropriate ending age and if the investment strategy is geared to produce what the plan requires. There is no question, however, that it is a riskier way forward than the faucet plan, as it is more complicated and there is less room for error.

If you choose to engage a professional to assist in bucket planning—and, frankly, you probably should as we mean it when we say there is little room for error—make sure you start with a plan and not a solution. Once the buckets are established, along with how much money needs to go in them today and the rate of return they need to get for however long they have to wait, then you can consider investment solutions to execute the plan. If the investment ideas come first, the cart is before the horse and you need to visit someone else.

8

Legacy Planning

If you have a retirement nest egg, there is a chance you will be leaving some of it behind. If you have a well-built faucet plan, you almost certainly will be leaving a financial legacy. If your bucket plan is built properly, it's planning for you to live longer than you likely will and there will be legacy money there as well. Most people think of dealing with this as a quick trip to a lawyer's office to draft a will, and while that is certainly a necessary component, that isn't all there is to it.

The place to begin is with the high-level conversation about what you want your financial legacy to be. If you are married, you and your spouse need to be on the same page. Some people really want to leave money to their children. Others want their children to make it on their own. Some people really want to financially support their place of worship or their favorite nonprofit organization. Others want their names to live on in legacy gifts as the names of buildings or parks. Some don't really care about any of this at all and just want to leave whatever they have left over at the end, if anything at all, to their kids and be done with it. There is no right answer, but your team of professionals needs to know what you want so they can help you get there.

THE ESTATE PLAN

Once you've sorted out where you want your wealth to go, you will need some written documentation to get it there in the form of an estate plan. This will require visiting a lawyer (not a website pretending to be a lawyer) and spending some time and money to get an actual estate plan that will work in your state.

Unfortunately, states are different and there is no such thing as a universal estate plan that will work everywhere. For example, in Georgia where we are based, a valid will must be witnessed by two people. A will with one witness or no witnesses isn't valid and won't be enforced by the courts. In Florida, however, a valid will requires three witnesses, which means if you get a will in Georgia with two witnesses and then move to Florida, that Georgia will just became useless to you. Every state is different. You must have a plan put together by a good lawyer in the state in which you live. If you move to another state, you need to get your estate plan reviewed by a lawyer there to be sure it will still work or to make modifications so it will be valid in the new state. It seems like it should be easier than this, but it isn't.

Once you've ended up in the right lawyer's office, something you should consider is whether to use a last will and testament or a living trust as the centerpiece of your plan. In fact, this should be the first question you ask your lawyer because there is a relatively uniform answer in some states. While there are not a lot of states where the trust is the normal estate planning vehicle, there are a few. If you happen to live in one of them, then the decision is largely made for you. The community property states and states that charge a percentage of your estate as their probate fee are typically trust states. If you live in one of those states, a simple will may not be the right answer. In the other states, however, it is an open question and you need to make the decision that is right for you.

We will forewarn you that putting the question of living trust versus will into your favorite internet search engine will garner some strong and fairly incendiary opinions. There is a school of thought out there among conspiracy theorists that everyone should have a trust because lawyers use wills to somehow control people's assets at their death. It's silly, but you'll find it. The truth is there are both advantages and disadvantages to a living trust arrangement.

The primary advantage of a living trust is that it will avoid the probate process if it is used properly. This is why the trust is the preferred method of estate planning in states where probate fees are oppressive. Avoiding probate can have advantages beyond saving probate fees. One of them is privacy. Probate proceedings, like all court proceedings, are matters of public record. Anyone can go pull a probate file in the clerk's office and take a look at it. Some people aren't concerned about this, but others find the invasion of privacy horrifying. If privacy is a concern for you, then that may be a reason to consider a living trust.

Another advantage to avoiding probate is speed. The probate process, even in relatively efficient states, is slow. It takes time to get in front of the court, run ads for creditors in the newspaper, and do some of the other technical things that many states require to fully probate an estate. Being named executor is not a glamorous job as anyone who has ever had to do it can attest. The living trust, if used properly, avoids this altogether because, once the grantor passes away, all the trustee has to do is administer the trust.

The final advantage to a living trust that we'll highlight is its ability to pull property together from multiple states. If you live in Georgia but own a condo on the beach in Florida and you pass away with a will, your executor will have to probate your estate in Georgia and then go to Florida, open an ancillary probate proceeding, and deal with the court there to get the condo transferred to your heirs. If your living trust owned the condo, the trip through the Florida probate courts could be avoided.

At this point, you are probably on board that a living trust is the way to go, but there are a couple of caveats. One advantage to a will is that it is a "set and forget" instrument. You have it drafted and then you put it on a shelf somewhere and, barring some huge life change, you don't think about it again. A living trust, on the other hand, comes to life as soon as you sign it and becomes something you have to live with and manage properly for it to do its job.

The issue we see most often with living trusts is that they aren't properly funded. Everything that would otherwise go through probate has to be put in your living trust. If you pass away with anything not in the trust that should be, the trust actually makes things worse. Now, your heirs will have to probate your "pour-over wills" to get everything into the trust and then administer the trust itself. What should be a one-step process becomes a two-step process. So, if you are going to have a living trust, you have to pay attention to it and make sure it stays properly funded.

Your house, for example, needs to be deeded into the trust if you really want it to work. That condo in Florida has to be deeded into the trust, which means hiring a Florida lawyer to help you. Bank accounts, investment accounts, business interests, etc., all have to get into the trust somehow. If you work with a good attorney, most of this will be dealt with when you draw up the trust, but lawyers don't call you to find out if you bought a new house or added another bank account. It's going to be your responsibility to be sure things stay in the trust once the initial drafting is done.

That said, not everything goes in the trust. You also have to know what things don't go in. Typically, what does not go in the trust are things that will pass outside of the probate process anyway. IRAs and other retirement accounts are the most obvious examples. You probably don't want to aim those in the trust, as you will typically lose their benefits if they go into the trust. This is where relying solely on a lawyer will sometimes get you in trouble. Knowing how retirement accounts work is what financial advisors are for, but many lawyers are loath to admit they don't know things, so they may have opinions that aren't particularly informed. Or they may simply not know much about the subject at all, which means they won't bring it up or they won't want to advise you on what to do.

Of course, there could be situations where you should aim an IRA at the trust despite the tax consequences. That's rare, but we've seen situations where personal family considerations trump good tax planning. The living trust gives you a lot of options, but it is also a device you have to start living with as soon as you create it. If you mishandle it, the living trust can create more headaches for your heirs than it solves.

The other downside to the living trust is the cost of creating it. It's hard to generalize about attorneys' fees, as you will find wide-ranging fees for the same services, but almost all lawyers will charge substantially more to draft a living trust than to draft a will, which is fair because they are more complicated and will require more time from the attorney. If you live in a state where the probate fees you are trying to avoid will be multiples of what it costs to create a trust, then the financial consideration is clear. If, however, you live in a state like Georgia where probate fees are low and relatively fixed, you won't necessarily be saving money in the long run with a living trust. That doesn't mean you shouldn't have a living trust, of course, it just means saving future probate costs shouldn't be a driving reason behind your decision.

ESTATE TAX PLANNING

Estate tax planning is such a Pandora's Box we hesitate to even bring it up, but estate taxes are out there and, while significant strides have been made during both the President Bush and President Obama years to minimize the number of people the tax impacts, it remains one of the tax code's most consequential taxes. If it happens to hit your estate, it will dramatically reduce the amount of money that makes it to your heirs.

As we sit here in 2016, each person has the ability to exempt about $5,000,000 from the estate tax, though this gets complicated if you've made taxable gifts during your life. If you are married, you and your spouse can combine your exemptions to reach a number more like $10,000,000. Of course, this all has a funny way of changing and changing often, so by the time you are reading this book it could be completely different. Make sure you ask a professional (or at least ask Google) what the estate tax exemption is in whatever year you need to know about.

If you have an estate tax exposure, you are going to need a good CPA, a good financial advisor, and a good lawyer to put together a plan. The difficulty you will run into is that these professionals tend to geek out about all of the nifty planning tools they can use. Before you know it, you are being lectured about how cool an "intentionally defective grantor retained interest trust" is, and your head is swimming.

The place to start with any sort of planning is at the highest level, no matter how complicated that planning may be. Once you identify what you are trying to do and conceptually how you want it done, you can leave it to the geeks to sort out exactly what tools get you there. At a very high level, there are really only two ways to deal with the estate tax. One is to accept the tax and figure out how to fund it so your heirs don't have to. The other is to try to minimize the tax by divesting yourself of assets before you pass away.

The funding idea is simpler, so we'll start there. One of the interesting advantages of life insurance is that, if you handle it properly [usually by having it purchased on your life by a trust that you create called an Irrevocable Life Insurance Trust (ILIT)], those life insurance proceeds will go to your heirs without coming into your estate. So, if you project that you will owe $1,000,000 in estate taxes, you could use an ILIT to purchase a $1,000,000 policy, and your heirs could use the life insurance proceeds to pay Uncle Sam and keep everything you are leaving them in your estate.

We're simplifying this concept a bit, of course, but based on your age, health, and wealth, sometimes this sort of planning can be made to work. The key is to see a good return on your investment in what is undoubtedly going to be an expensive life insurance policy. There are ways to project a policy's rate of return and see if this strategy is sensible. Life insurance agents love this idea, as you might imagine, but there are situations when this is the best way forward. If you happen to have a lot of wealth tied up in hard-to-liquidate assets, like real estate or business interests, figuring out how to fund the estate tax is critical to preserving your wealth. A fire sale on your business or real estate holdings to raise cash for Uncle Sam is not usually a good plan.

Of course, funding the estate tax with life insurance isn't for everyone. Health and age can make it impossible even if you like the idea. Your other primary planning path is to make your estate smaller before you die, and that means divesting yourself of some of your assets. Sounds easy enough, but this is where you're going to need some geeks! You see, the IRS is well on to this plan, so you can't just give stuff away.

We apologize in advance for this technical detour, but to see why you can't just give things away, you need a better understanding of the current $5,000,000 per person estate tax exemption. In tax speak, it really isn't an exemption at all. It's a tax credit that is enough to fund the taxes owed on a $5,000,000 estate called the "unified credit."

The other side of the estate tax coin is the gift tax, and it's the gift tax that prevents you from gaining an advantage by simply giving your stuff away before you die. If you want to give away large taxable gifts and not pay taxes, you must draw down your unified credit. So, however much of the credit you use during your life to make gifts is deducted from the amount of credit you have available to use on your estate when you pass. This two-sided taxation on gifts and estates is why you can't just give your stuff away the day before you pass and dodge the estate tax. The IRS will get its tax either way.

So to reduce your estate tax exposure, you need a smaller estate. However, it isn't going to be quite as easy as just giving things away. This is where your professionals are going to have to help. Our caution to you is that you must understand that when they say you are giving things away, you really are *giving them away*. You cannot get them back. If you form any sort of irrevocable trust—no matter what flavor—and you put something in it, you cannot change your mind and you will never get what you put in back out.

All of the various divesting strategies are way more than you want to read about in this book, but we'll highlight a couple of common ones. The first and easiest one you can actually implement without any professional help. The IRS allows you to give away a certain amount of money each year under the annual gift tax exclusion. As of 2016, you can give away up to $14,000 to a person without paying a gift tax or using your unified credit. So, if you have two children, you could give them each $14,000. If you are married, your spouse can do that as well, so you would give each of them $28,000. This would effectively get $56,000 out of your estate this year.

Of course, if you have a taxable estate, you are worth millions and this amount of money isn't going to make a huge difference, but it's a good starting strategy and there are ways to enhance it. The obvious one is to do it every year. If you can put together several years of these gifts, you will begin to reduce the size of your estate more substantially. The other is to give them things other than cash. If you give away $56,000 worth of a good stock, for example, you are not only giving away the $56,000 it is worth today, you are also getting its future growth out of your estate.

After utilizing the annual gift tax exclusion, the strategies are going to get a lot more complicated. One that many people like is a Charitable Remainder Trust (CRT). The idea here is you donate money to a CRT, the CRT pays you some sort of income stream back while you are alive, and then whatever is left in the CRT at your death goes to a nonprofit charitable organization. Sometimes this is a good way to derive the income you want from your investments while mitigating estate taxes and supporting a charity that is important to you all at once.

If charitable giving is particularly important to you, a family foundation is something you also might consider. You've no doubt heard of the Bill and Melinda Gates Foundation, the Tiger Woods Foundation, and others like them. Those are family foundations and represent a form of charitable giving that can have estate tax planning benefits. There are also donor advised funds out there that accomplish a similar goal with less expense and complication than you'll find in forming your own family foundation.

After charitable giving, there are several strategies that focus on trying to give away the present value of assets so their growth can occur outside of the estate. Business interests and real estate interests often work well in these strategies. This sort of planning can all get very complex, but if you are facing a large estate tax bill, the complexity may be worthwhile. As always, though, our advice is to find someone to quarterback the team. You'll need a good CPA, a good lawyer, and a good financial advisor and someone needs to be sure they are communicating with each other.

A book could be written on all of the various estate tax planning ideas (though we're not sure who would really want to read it). The good news is the estate tax doesn't impact most families, and, when it does, some of the basic giving strategies and charitable strategies are enough to solve it. If you have enough wealth that you actually need to know what an "intentionally defective grantor retained interest trust" is, then look on the bright side: that's a great problem to have!

9

Protection Planning

We aren't big on insurance. We think it's oversold by insurance agents and a lot of people end up with a lot more of it than they need. That said, the public and media are often more down on insurance than they should be because they know it can be oversold by unscrupulous life insurance agents. Insurance is simply a tool through which you can transfer certain risks away from yourself and onto an insurance company, in exchange for payments called premiums.

Consider your homeowners insurance. There is a risk that a fire could break out in your home and burn it to the ground. If it did, it would likely cost you hundreds of thousands of dollars to rebuild your house and, all the while, your current mortgage would still have to be repaid. Most people couldn't afford this catastrophe even if they were relatively wealthy. So, rather than bear this risk themselves, people accept the risk of paying the mortgage and sell the risk of replacing the house to their homeowners insurance company. In exchange for a relatively small amount of money each year, the homeowner doesn't have to worry about the cost of rebuilding the house because the insurance company will pay to rebuild the house instead.

This idea of selling particular risks to an insurance company is the underlying concept of any insurance. So, when should you sell a risk to an insurance company? The easy answer is to sell the risk when you can't afford to cover it yourself or when the insurance is so cheap relative to the prospect of loss that "self-insuring" the risk would be a poor decision. To help you better understand various insurances this way, consider the chart below.

Type of Insurance	**Risk Transferred to the Insurer**
Homeowners Insurance	Risk of significant damage to the home
Auto Insurance	Risk of damage caused in an auto accident
Life Insurance	Risk of not living long enough to build the wealth your family needs
Annuity	Risk of outliving your money
Disability Insurance	Risk you will become disabled and unable to earn money by working
Long-Term Care Insurance	Risk that a long stay in a nursing home or similar facility will cause you to outlive your money
Health Insurance	Risk that a major medical event will create medical bills you could not afford to pay
Hole-In-One Insurance	Risk that someone will actually make a hole-in-one on the hole where a golf course is offering a free car to anyone who makes a hole-in-one (Yes, this is real.)

In all of these instances, someone is buying insurance with the intent of transferring the risk to an insurance company, so they do not have to bear that risk themselves. The question for the consumer of insurance is what risks to keep versus what risks to sell and how much is it worth paying for the protection. A good advisor can help you here, but insurance contracts pay commissions (and sometimes large ones), so make sure you understand the advice you are getting.

HOME AND AUTO INSURANCE

State laws require you to have auto insurance and mortgage companies require you to have homeowners, so there is not a lot of decision-making to be done about whether to own it. The bigger question is how much. In our experience, most people are underinsured in both of these areas. Home and auto are among the cheapest insurances you can buy because there is almost nothing about them that is specific to you. You don't take a driving test to find out how much your auto insurance will cost, and no one tests your DIY skills before giving you homeowners insurance.

These insurances run perfectly well on what insurers call "the law of large numbers." They insure enough drivers and enough homes that they can predict their claim risk with great precision and that brings the cost down for everyone. Do they cheat with the statistics to justify charging more? Of course they do (but that's another book). That aside, this is still very cheap insurance and there is no reason for you to try to make it cheaper by underinsuring yourself.

Pull your auto insurance out and review it. If you caused a big accident and someone sued you, do you really have enough insurance to cover it? If not, you need more. Here is an even better question. If someone who had little or no insurance of their own hit you and hurt you badly, do you have the money to pay for all of that yourself? Would you want to? Wouldn't you want some recovery for your pain and suffering? Then look at your underinsured/uninsured motorist limits. A lot of people don't realize their policy even covers this, but it does. It's important to make sure these limits are enough to bail you out of the type of situation where a drunk, uninsured guy driving without a license and without insurance hits you.

If these limits are low through inattention or because your agent sold you the policy based on making your rates lower, fix them at once. If they are low because you're cheap, you need to rethink your strategy. You don't buy insurance for the day you pay the premium; you buy insurance for the day the drunk driver falls asleep and plows head on into you. The risk is real and its potential cost is enormous. For a few more dollars per month, you can transfer the risk to the insurer who is much better equipped to handle it.

Now pull out your homeowners policy and take a look at that. There are lots of internal limits you should consider in this policy too, but the one we see most often ignored is the replacement value for the home. If you bought your house 10 years ago, the value of your home for insurance purposes was likely set at that time. If you haven't thought twice about your homeowners insurance since then, that replacement value for your house is likely still the same as it was 10 years ago. It's time to update it. If your house burns down, you want to collect what it's worth, not what it used to be worth.

Your last assignment is to call your home and auto agent and ask them to price out an umbrella policy. An umbrella policy is extra insurance that can be added to your home and auto insurance in the event you really encounter a big problem. We've seen $1,000,000 umbrella policies for less than $150 per year.

If you will put a little effort into your home and auto policies, you will likely be able to right-size all of your limits and dramatically improve your coverage for relatively little money. Don't get carried away, of course. Pushing the premiums past what you can afford is clearly not the goal, but we find that most people who have amassed decent-sized nest eggs are underinsured for these basic risks. A good advisor or insurance agent can help you figure out how much insurance you really need, but in the area of home and auto, err on the side of having more than less.

LIFE INSURANCE

Do you need it all? That is the big question as you approach retirement, and the answer is that it depends. As you consider the question, keep in mind the risk exchange concept from the chart above. Life insurance is insurance against the risk of you not living long enough. Would your death in the very near future cause significant financial harm to your family or is your wealth largely built at this point? That is really the question.

In general, your need for life insurance follows a bell curve through your adult life. As a young adult, you don't really need it. As a married adult with children trying to build your wealth, you absolutely need it, as your premature death is a major financial risk for your family. As a retiree, your need for it typically goes back down—as, at this point, your wealth is largely built and your death is not a major financial risk for your family. Since this is the typical evolution of things, as a retiree, you should be skeptical of any suggestion that you need life insurance because you probably don't. You may find, however, that you want it, and that is a different matter entirely.

The primary purpose of life insurance is to allocate the risk of you dying too soon to an insurance company and away from your family. As you age, that risk decreases and the need to transfer it decreases too. Unlike most other insurances, however, life insurance has some uses as a planning tool. Why? Because it is the only insurance we know of where the insured event will always happen.

Your house may never burn down. You may never be an in auto accident. You may never need to stay in a nursing home. You may never become disabled. Because of this, risk transfer is the only use for any of these insurances. You will, however, pass away. Sorry to be a downer, but we will all die eventually. Because of that, the risk the life insurance company is accepting will ultimately come to pass. With the known outcome of the risk, life insurance can have an investment/planning function based on a known payout at an unknown time in the future.

To be clear, if you plan to use life insurance this way, it is going to be very expensive, as it is obviously not lost on the insurer that they will eventually have to pay their policy limits to someone. If you buy a term policy when you are 28 that will last for 30 years, it's going to be very cheap (assuming you are reasonably healthy), because the insurer knows that while you will certainly die eventually, you are unlikely to do so by age 58. Since the insurer doesn't expect to pay out on the policy, it charges you less for it. If you buy a permanent policy when you are 60, the insurer knows it will pay out its limits eventually, and then the math for the insurer gets very different.

So, why would you buy an expensive life insurance policy when you are past the point in your life when transferring the financial risk of your premature death is important? The answer is because the payout your family can count on from the insurer is of some value in your overall estate planning. We covered one possible reason a chapter ago and that is to fund estate taxes.

Another reason could be to create liquidity in your estate. If you will be passing a lot of real estate to your heirs that you want them to keep, for example, they are going to need some cash to maintain the properties, keep them insured, pay the property taxes, etc. If you don't have the cash to pass them, a life insurance policy is a potential solution to the problem.

We've also seen people decide to use life insurance to insure a particular gift at their death. We have a client who has purchased a large life insurance policy in an irrevocable life insurance trust for the benefit of his favorite charity. He knows that the charity will get exactly the gift he wants them to get no matter what happens in the rest of his estate.

We have another client couple that has approached the same issue from the other direction and purchased two life insurance policies, one for each of their children. Those life insurance policies represent the children's inheritance and their estate plan leaves everything else they own to various charities they wish to support.

All of these can be good strategies, and they can also be expensive and unnecessary ideas the mostly benefit the insurance agent. The key is to approach the idea as an investment and compare it to the obvious other option, which is to pay the "premiums" to yourself. If you can afford a $20,000 per year insurance premium, then you can also afford to put $20,000 per year into an investment account. The question is which option is more beneficial to you. The way you will begin to assess this is to look hard at the internal rate of return on the life insurance policy, which will be presented to you in the illustration before you make a purchasing decision.

The illustration is going to show you that, based on some assumed rate of return inside the policy, your death benefit will be a certain amount each year along the way. This gets complicated without having an illustration to show you, but just know you'll see one and there are a couple of things to look for.

One is that you want to be sure the illustration is illustrating a reasonable-looking rate of return. We've seen some policy illustrations where the rate of return in the policy is 12 percent per year and, suddenly, the illustration says this is the greatest investment ever made. All insurance products are expensive. If you are putting money into a variable policy that is carrying 5 percent or better in fees and costs of insurance, do you really think you'll see a 12 percent return year over year in the policy (which would be more like a real life 17 percent return)? No way.

Illustrations usually show what happens at a 0 percent return (it crashes and you'd never buy it), what happens at a borderline silly rate of return like 12 percent, and then something more reasonable in the middle. Focus on the middle number, but make sure it is reasonable. Your agent can run almost any number he or she wants in there. Make sure it is a sensible one that accounts for the fees and costs of the policy. You want to see an illustration with a reasonably likely outcome, not a pie-in-the-sky one.

The other major thing to look for is whether any of the death benefit is guaranteed and, if so, up to what age. A lot of permanent policies eventually turn off the guaranteed death benefit and give you a death benefit related to the cash value built inside the policy through your premiums. There is always a bet against yourself in a life insurance policy about how long you'll live. If you are 60 today and you pass away at age 104, you'd probably be better off just investing money you would have spent on premiums. If you pass away at 75, the life insurance policy will likely be a great investment. The illustration is your view into how good an investment it might be and at what age it begins to lose its value as an investment, which is why you need a good, honest illustration.

Life insurance can certainly be a useful planning tool in your retirement, particularly to accomplish giving or inheritance goals. Just know that if you plan to consider using it this way, you are really looking at it more as an investment and less as a risk transfer tool. While it will always have some risk transfer value, this probably isn't a good strategy for you if the policy doesn't make sense as an investment.

LONG-TERM CARE

Statistically, the greatest threat to your retirement is a long-term care stay. In fact, someone turning 65 today has a 70 percent chance of spending some portion of their remaining years in a long-term care situation, according the U.S. Department of Health and Human Services.[4] That long-term care stay is increasingly often in the home with some sort of hired in-home caregiver, but it is a long-term care stay nonetheless.

Long-term care costs vary, of course, depending on what sort of care you need, but they are expensive no matter how they are provided. According to the 2010 study by the U.S. Department of Health and Human Services, the average cost of just a semi-private room in a nursing home in the United States was $6,235 per month. That's nearly $75,000 per year.[5] With women averaging 3.7 years in long-term care, your nest egg could be looking at a $275,000 draw down in a short amount of time.[6]

Long-term care costs are, without question, a major risk to your retirement nest egg. The question is whether you should keep this risk or transfer it to an insurer. Unfortunately, we have to begin that analysis with a reality check. Insurers have sprinted away from this risk in recent years with the spiraling

4 http://longtermcare.gov/the-basics/how-much-care-will-you-need

5 http://longtermcare.gov/costs-how-to-pay/costs-of-care

6 http://longtermcare.gov/the-basics/how-much-care-will-you-need

costs of long-term care and the sheer volume of claimants. The insurers that have remained in the business of providing long-term care insurance have dramatically increased the cost of their products to better protect themselves from the volume of claims. All of which is a long way of saying you may not have the option of insuring this risk, even if you want to.

The question of whether it is a risk you can keep is a function of your nest egg and how much of your nest egg you are spending. If your nest egg could survive a $250,000 or so hit over the last three years of your life, then you can afford to keep the risk. In our experience, most good faucet plans can survive the long-term care hit. Bucket plans, on the other hand, are typically more fragile, and those are the plans that can be completely derailed by a long-term care event.

If you really feel like a long-term care event would derail your retirement, then explore some long-term care insurance, by all means. Just go in with low expectations and your eyes wide open. A good policy with an affordable premium is going to be hard to find. The younger you are, the better chance you have. If you just happen to be reading this in your early 50s, you are actually in the best position you'll ever be in to buy long-term care, so you may want to look into it.

We've decided not to try and unpack annuities and life insurance policies with long-term care riders here because there is too much ground to cover in a book. Just know that they exist and could be an option for you. They are expensive and they are not all the same, so be sure you are working with someone you trust and be sure you fully understand the product before jumping into it. In our experience, if you can afford to insure yourself against a long-term care event through an annuity, you can usually afford to insure yourself without the annuity. Annuities do have some "sleep well at night" features for some people, though.

ANNUITIES

We can't put it off any longer. We've danced around them, but we would do you a disservice to simply ignore the most controversial tool in the retirement planner's box: the annuity. Annuities come in many different flavors. The annuities of today are very different than the ones of 10 years ago, which are different still than the ones of decades ago that really gave annuities a bad name in the first place. Therefore, we will attempt to provide some clarity around what annuities can and cannot do without too much editorializing about them. The truth is they are a tool like anything else, and if the tool is applied to the right problem, it can be effective. A hammer works quite well if you need to drive a nail. It is a lousy tool, however, for cutting wood. The real problem isn't whether the hammer is good or bad. The problem is that if you are in the business of selling hammers, everything starts to look like a nail, and that is where annuities can get in trouble.

Most, though not all, annuities are sold through insurance agencies and/or broker dealer networks. Therefore, they offer commissions as compensation for selling them. The longer the annuity contract, often the higher the commission. So, there is no question that for someone who really likes to sell things, annuities provide a great mechanism for making a living. Because of this, they have been sold far too often to far too many people who may or may not have needed them, thus earning their reputation as good for the broker and bad for the client. Our goal here is to lay aside all of that baggage for a moment and actually consider the tool itself, not the people who sell them.

An annuity is a form of insurance. Recall that all forms of insurance transfer risk from you to an insurance company. Annuities transfer the risk of you outliving your money to an insurance company in exchange for a premium. In accepting that risk, annuity companies are also agreeing to accept the risk of the stock market going down. These are significant risks and no insurance company would take this risk for free, so it should not surprise you that annuities are somewhat expensive.

Annuities typically accept the risk of you outliving your money by guaranteeing you a lifetime income stream. Remember our faucet plan? Many annuities offer a form of the faucet plan. They promise to pay a certain percentage (usually 4 percent or so) of the amount you put in the annuity back to you, per year for the rest of your life. Now, we said that running out of money shouldn't really be an option in a good faucet plan and we meant it, but our saying that doesn't satisfy everyone. You can certainly model a couple of ill-timed 2008-type years into your faucet plan and show how you could run out of money. The annuity eliminates that risk. As long as the annuity company remains in business, they will pay your income no matter what happens to your principal balance.

The annuities that agree to pay you an income stream for life and accept the risk of investing your money are called variable annuities. Those annuities will put your money into the stock market and if the market really goes up, you could see some small upward adjustments in your income as the base upon which your withdrawal rate grows. If the market drops, however, your income will typically stay the same. And if your annuity runs out of money altogether somehow, the annuity company will keep paying as long as you live. This deal isn't cheap, and this is certainly not how you maximize the growth in your investments over time. But if the market really worries you and you need some guarantees for a peaceful retirement, these annuities can be an option.

The downside of variable annuities is that once you invest, you typically cannot take your money back out until the end of the "surrender period." How long that lasts depends on what sort of contract your agent sold you. Most annuities come in 5-, 7-, and 10-year flavors. The longer the contract, the richer the guarantees from the annuity company, but the longer before you can change your mind.

The other broad category of annuities are fixed annuities. These do not participate in the stock market and, instead, offer you some guarantees about your principal. They are tied to interest rates, which are historically low (as of this writing in 2016), making them not particularly compelling products. In higher rate times, however, they have promised to increase your investment by a few percentage points each year until the product matures.

The downside pointed to most often by those who really oppose annuities is the cost. In our minds, the cost is a consideration, but not the biggest one.

After all, the annuity company is taking some fairly significant risks off of your shoulders, and they are going to have to be compensated to do it. The biggest issue we see in annuities is liquidity. Once you put your money in, you cannot take it out for some period of time. And to fully realize the benefits of the annuity, you typically need to leave the money alone for some period of time. If you put too much of your wealth into annuities, you don't have money to dip into for the next cruise, a new car, or whatever else you want to do.

If you plan to make annuities part of your retirement plan, there are couple of rules we think you should follow. The first is that no more than half of your liquid net worth should be in an annuity. For example, if you have $200,000 in savings, no more than $100,000 should be in an annuity. Frankly, if you can make it less than that and still accomplish your goals, that would be even better. You must keep liquidity in your retirement plan and you cannot do it if you put too much money into an annuity.

Many annuities, particularly variable annuities, offer some benefits that come from putting the money into the annuity and then holding off on taking any income for some period of time. Make sure you understand what those benefits are and how long you need to hold off on taking income before you turn the income on. A lot of those benefits cost money in the form of a rider. If you buy a rider, make sure you don't do something that negates what the rider was supposed to do for you. The annuity company won't refund the cost of the rider.

Finally, make sure you are happy with the underlying investments in any variable annuity. Part of what your advisor is doing in selling you an annuity is outsourcing the investments to the annuity company. Annuity companies use mutual funds for the most part and some of them seem to be better at this than others. You want to be sure you are going to get some reasonable rates of return relative to the stock market. You can't usually pick the funds yourself, though sometimes you can, but you do want to see some track record in the company's models.

In our view, annuities are tools that are neither good nor bad in and of themselves. They are what they are, and if you have a problem the annuity solves, you shouldn't feel bad about owning one. The primary problem they solve is the "sleep well at night" problem. If you need to know that a check of a certain amount is going to show up in your mailbox every month for the rest of your life, an annuity might be for you.

But annuities are absolutely not for everyone. If you want to maximize your nest egg during retirement, annuities are not for you. If you can handle the ups and downs of the stock market, annuities are not for you. And, to be quite frank, if you have a lot more money than you will ever spend, annuities are not for you. You just don't need them.

If you really want to explore annuities, make sure you are doing it with an advisor that has more tools in the toolbox than just the annuity. Annuities are seductive and they are often sold by hardcore salesmen who know a lot about their products and very little about investing in general, the stock market, or anything else that might help you decide if the product is right for you. An annuity is never the only option. There is always another way to accomplish whatever goal you are being told the annuity will accomplish. The annuity may be the right way for you, but don't decide until you've considered the other ways also.

10

Live Life and Have Fun

Retirement is a life-altering event. Whether it alters your life for the better or for the worse has a lot to do with how you choose to manage it. The peace of mind that comes with a sound financial plan that is carefully knitted to a well-crafted investment plan will go a long way toward removing the financial obstacles between you and the retirement you deserve.

You'll get the rest of the way by understanding that success in retirement has nothing to do with how you lived while working. Some people save enough to fully maintain their standard of living in retirement, and if you are one of those, you should be commended for a job well done. But that was success while working, not while retired. Success in retirement is building a plan that balances your aspirations for a perfect retirement against what can realistically be attained based on your savings and income, and then living that plan to the fullest.

So build a plan, put it in place, and get about the serious business of enjoying your retirement. You've earned it!

11

Talk to Your Kids

We have one last assignment for you. There is a retirement crisis brewing in this country that has received relatively little media attention, but it must be addressed and soon. We all know that most Americans retiring today have not saved enough to maintain their standard of living. In fact, we covered a lot of those statistics in the beginning of this book. The good news is that many of them have some type of pension, albeit much smaller than what their parents may have had, and they have Social Security, which at the moment will sustain a reasonable standard of living.

The people retiring today had to deal with a major shift in retirement planning during the course of their careers. When they began work, retirement was a pension or similar defined benefit plan. Somewhere along the way, they really needed to embrace the 401(k) and take it upon themselves to save for retirement. Some did and some didn't, but it's easy to understand how many missed the importance of the transition.

The working adults of today don't have this excuse. They joined the workforce as part of the 401(k) generation. And many of us Generation Xers watched our parents fall victim to age-based downsizing and loss of pensions. Combine that life experience with the general skepticism that Social Security will exist in a meaningful way when Generation X retires, and you would think everyone working today would be saving like crazy for retirement.

The truth is very much the opposite. More than 30 percent of people working today report they have not saved *at all* for retirement. Never mind not saving enough, nearly a third of workers haven't started saving at all! And lest you think the other 70 percent are in good shape, 60 percent of all workers report that, while they may have saved in the past, they are not currently saving for retirement.

So what is going on? There is no question that the general economy turned on younger workers in 2008. And while many are now employed again, many are underemployed or working for less money than before. When this happens, retirement savings is probably the first thing to go. It shouldn't be, but it is.

It is also true that many successful Generation Xers are very cynical about the current debt of the U.S. government and cynical about rising tax rates in the future. Because of that, we have clients who are choosing to pay taxes today and save money outside of 401(k)s or other qualified retirement plans, which takes them out of the statistical pool of people saving into retirement plans.

So, there are at least these reasons, and perhaps others, to explain why some current workers are not saving for retirement, but we are very skeptical that this explains it for most of today's workers. The problem seems more pervasive than that, and statistics don't suggest Generation X was behaving very differently before 2008. The most telling statistic is that more than half of workers report they have no idea how much money they need to save for retirement *and* have never tried to figure it out.

The problem seems to be that today's workers are just sticking their heads in the sand when it comes to retirement. They have to know they need to save, just like everyone today has to know that cigarettes are really bad for you, but they are just choosing not to accept that reality. At least smokers have a physical addiction to deal with. Workers today are just being downright irresponsible, and someone has to let them know how this show ends.

As discussed earlier in the book, it's estimated that approximately 30 percent of today's adults are contributing to their parents' care. And most of those parents have at least some sort of pension and they get Social Security.

What is this going to look like when those parents are the 401(k) generation that didn't bother to save for retirement? And how ugly is this going to be if Social Security benefits are less meaningful in the future than they are today?

Workers today absolutely have to change their attitudes toward the future. Hoping it all somehow works out isn't much of a plan. The truth is that most workers who make a reasonable amount of money can actually allocate some money toward a retirement plan, adjust their income tax withholdings to reflect the plan contributions, and have their take-home pay stay the same. Why wouldn't they do this? *Everyone* with a W2 wage should be saving for retirement habitually from every paycheck. Even if it's just tens of dollars each check, it's better than nothing.

This is a little more complicated for small-business owners who don't have predictable pay, but the good news for small-business owners is they have a whole host of retirement and financial planning options available to them that are not available to salaried employees, and they have much greater opportunity to tailor a retirement plan for the business that suits their needs. We work with a number of clients who own small businesses who take advantage of things like Self Employed Pensions (SEPs) and SIMPLE IRAs to help fund retirement and reduce their tax burden.

Today's workers simply must be made to understand the importance of saving for retirement. They must also understand that it is *never* too late to start saving. We have many successful retiree clients who didn't get serious about saving for retirement until they were in their 50s. That isn't ideal, but it's a lot better than nothing. And if you save aggressively and can get some wind at your back in the stock market, you can create a reasonable nest egg in a relatively short amount of time.

So please encourage your kids, your nieces and nephews, and anyone else you find to start saving and start doing it *now*. Saving isn't about how much money you make, it's about discipline and forming good financial habits. One of our most successful retiree clients began his work life in the Army and then went on to be a package delivery driver for a major package company. He made decent money over the course of his career, but certainly a lot less than many of our other clients. But, in his Army days, he formed the habit of setting 10 percent of his take-home pay aside from every paycheck. He did this religiously for his entire working life. Forty years later, he has a seven-figure nest egg and is looking at condos in Costa Rica.

We said earlier that it's almost impossible to retire to a grander lifestyle than the one you had while working, but there is an exception to every rule, and this guy is one of those exceptions. He is the hallmark for what living within your means and being a disciplined saver can do for your retirement.

Anyone retiring today can have a successful retirement, but we are skeptical that will remain true in a generation. Unless Social Security is not only saved, but substantially retooled, some success at saving while working is going to be required for a successful retirement. We constantly tout the success of our favorite retired package delivery driver when working with our younger clients to identify the annual retirement savings they need to bank today to have the retirement they desire. Of course, we are preaching to the choir, because they are already saving and planning their finances or they wouldn't be working with us.

So please help us spread the word to the younger generation. We truly believe that *anyone* retiring today can be successful in retirement. But we doubt that is going to be true forever, and the time to start planning for that future is today.

About the Author

M. Andrew Riddle lives in Marietta, Georgia, with his wife and their two daughters. The owner of Rev Capital LLC—a "fee-only" advisory firm that builds custom portfolios for retirees—Riddle has helped many people through the financial part of retirement and learned about the pitfalls that await retirees as well as what a successful retirement looks like.

A licensed attorney and former partner at an Atlanta law firm, Riddle has received many awards: 5 Star Wealth Manager, from *Atlanta Magazine*; Top Lawyers in Georgia, from *American Lawyer Media*; and Super Lawyers "Rising Star," from *Georgia Super Lawyers Magazine*.

Made in the USA
Monee, IL
04 November 2026

67377682R00046